Eclipse Fever!

**Fun, Activities and Fascinating Facts:
A children's guide to the 1999 Eclipse**

by Antonia Thomas

© 1999 Planetesimal® Publishing Limited

All rights reserved. No part of this publication may be reproduced, stored in a retrieval system, or transmitted in any form or by any means, electronic, mechanical, photocopying, recording or otherwise, without the prior permission of the publishers.

ISBN 0-9534947-1-3

Published by
Planetesimal® Publishing Limited
PO Box No. 147
Paignton, Devon TQ4 6YH

Printed by The Devonshire Press Ltd,
Torquay, Devon TQ2 7NX

Disclaimer of Liability

Neither Planetesimal® Publishing Limited, its employees nor anyone involved with the creation, production or distribution of this book, shall be liable for any loss or damage arising from the use or inability to use the information printed herein.

Planetesimal® Publishing Limited
would like to thank the following for their help, enthusiasm
and valuable contributions, without whom this book would
not have been possible.

Information, diagrams, photographs:
Fred Espenac and NASA/GSFC from RP1398
Photographs Copyright © Hiram Clawson

AMOUNT OF ECLIPSE COVERAGE ACROSS GREAT BRITAIN

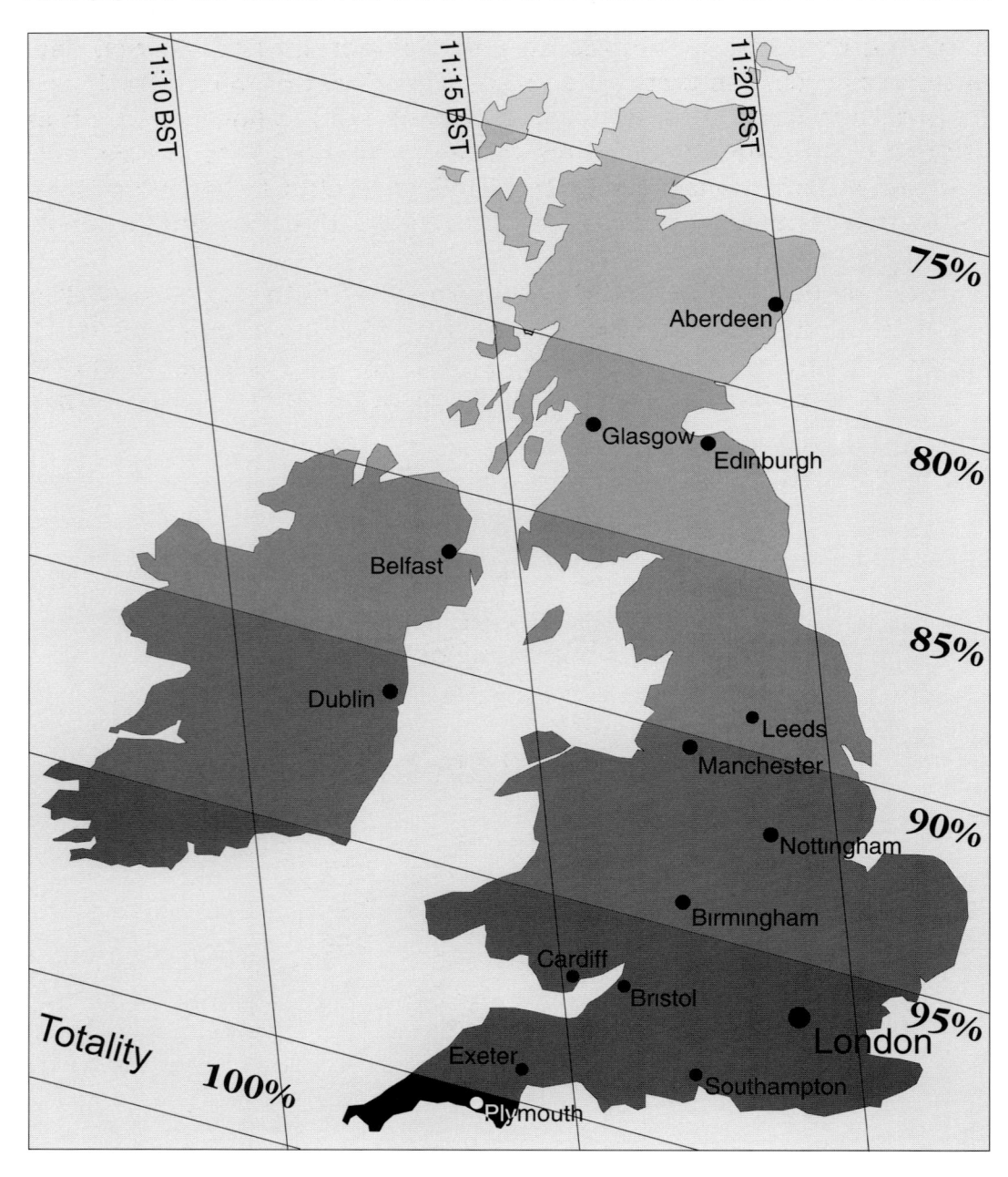

Eclipse Fever!

The 11th of August, 1999, is going to be a very important and exciting day. It's the date of a total solar eclipse that will be seen from Great Britain. An eclipse is when the moon passes in front of the sun and blocks out all the light, so that it seems as though it were night time – right in the middle of the day! A total solar eclipse is a very rare event. In fact, the last time a total eclipse could be seen from Great Britain was in 1927, when 3 million people travelled to the north of England to see it.

The 1999 total eclipse will be seen over Cornwall, South Devon and the Isles of Scilly, right in the middle of the summer holidays. Millions of people will be there to see it, travelling in trains, cars and buses and filling up the hotels and camp sites. Some people will even take special boats and planes to travel along the path of the eclipse!

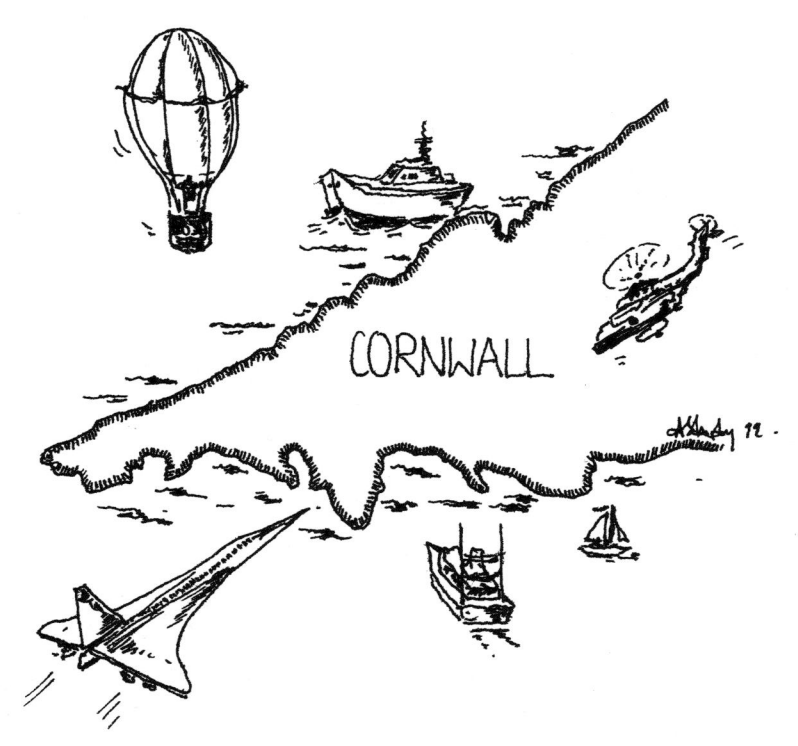

It will be an especially exciting time for children living or on holiday in the south west of England. They will be able to see one of nature's most exciting events in action. This book has been written to help you get the most out of the total eclipse, whether you're in the south west of England on 11th August, or whether you're watching a partial eclipse from elsewhere. Full of puzzles, activities and fascinating facts, Eclipse Fever will tell you:-

- what you can expect to see and should look for

- what equipment will come in useful (including some things you can make yourself)

- why eclipses happen

- what eclipses have meant to people in the past.

So get reading, writing, drawing and making! Happy sky-watching!

CONTENTS

Astronomy, Science and Stuff Like That . . .	1
How are you doing so far? – worksheet	8
Getting Ready for the Eclipse	10
What do we see during a Total Solar Eclipse?	15
Your Eclipse record	16
How much have you remembered? – worksheet	26
Superstitions, Myths and Legends	29
Puzzle Page	35
Dot to Dot	36
Answers	37
Glossary	39

Teachers may photocopy worksheets

ASTRONOMY, SCIENCE, AND STUFF LIKE THAT . . .

A solar eclipse happens when the moon comes between the sun and the earth and casts a shadow on the earth's surface. A *total* eclipse is when the face of the sun is covered entirely.

But hang on a minute! If you imagine the sun as the size of a football, then the earth would be about the same size as a pea, and the moon, spinning around it, would be no bigger than the head of a pin.

So how can something the size of a pinhead block out a football? Sounds crazy, doesn't it? But you can see how it works for yourself very simply.

Stand still somewhere outside, and find an object to look at quite a long way away. A tree or a car will do. Now bring your thumb up in front of your eyes. It's quite easy to block out a tree or a car with your thumb isn't it? Well, that's exactly what happens with an eclipse. Although the sun is very much bigger than the moon (about 400 times bigger) it's also much further away (about 400 times further). So when we look at the moon, it seems to be almost exactly the same size as the sun. And that's how we have eclipses!

Pathways through Space

There's much more to a total eclipse than a lucky coincidence. To understand why eclipses happen when they do, we have to look at how the sun, moon and earth move around each other.

"PHEW! NEVER MIND THE EARTH – MY HEAD'S SPINNING!"

The moon moves on a path around the earth called an orbit. One complete orbit of the earth takes 25 hours. At the same time, the earth is spinning round, taking 24 hours to make a complete turn – one day. And at the same time as that is happening, the earth is moving along a much larger orbit around the sun, which takes 365 days to complete.

When we look up into the sky, we see the sun and moon travelling along the same path. But because they are travelling at different speeds, every 29 days the sun "catches up" with the moon. Usually we don't notice this, because the sun normally passes above or below the moon. But when the sun passes behind the moon, we have an eclipse!

Here is a diagram of the moon's orbit around the earth, and the earth's orbit around the sun. Where do you think the moon has to be for an eclipse to happen? Draw it in.

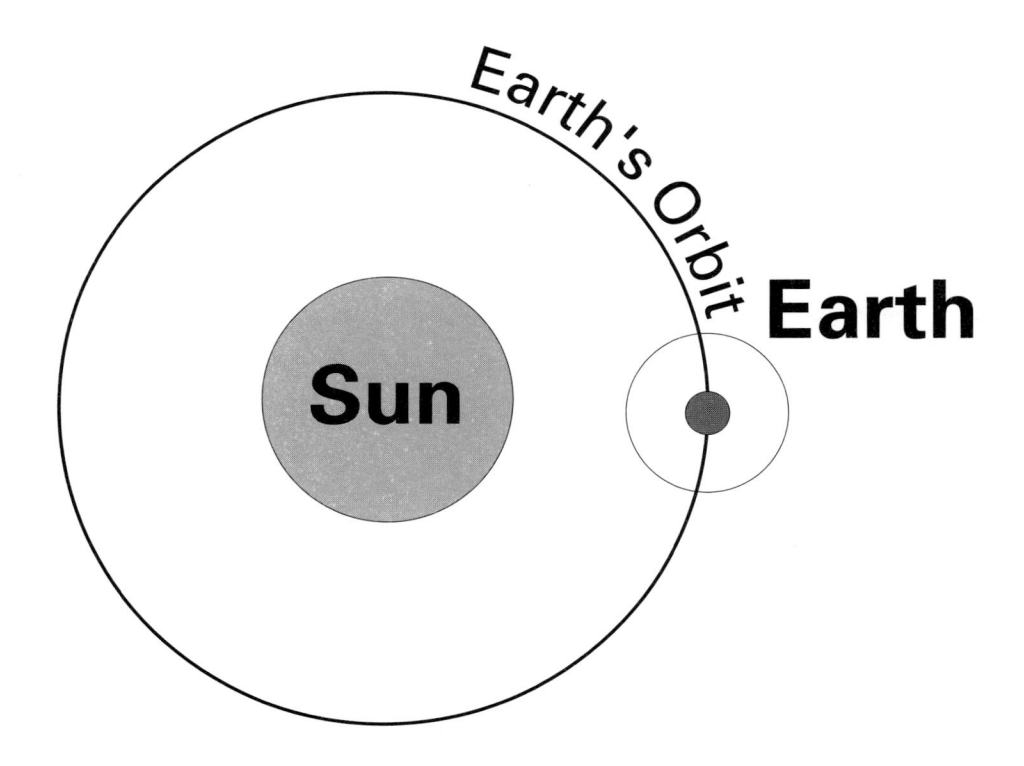

3

Different Kinds of Eclipses

On 11th August 1999 some parts of the world, including the south west of England, will be able to see a **total** eclipse. But this isn't the only kind of eclipse that we see on earth.

If you look at the diagram below you will see that during an eclipse the moon has not one, but two shadows. The paler, outer shadow is called a **penumbra**, and the darker, inner shadow is called an **umbra**.

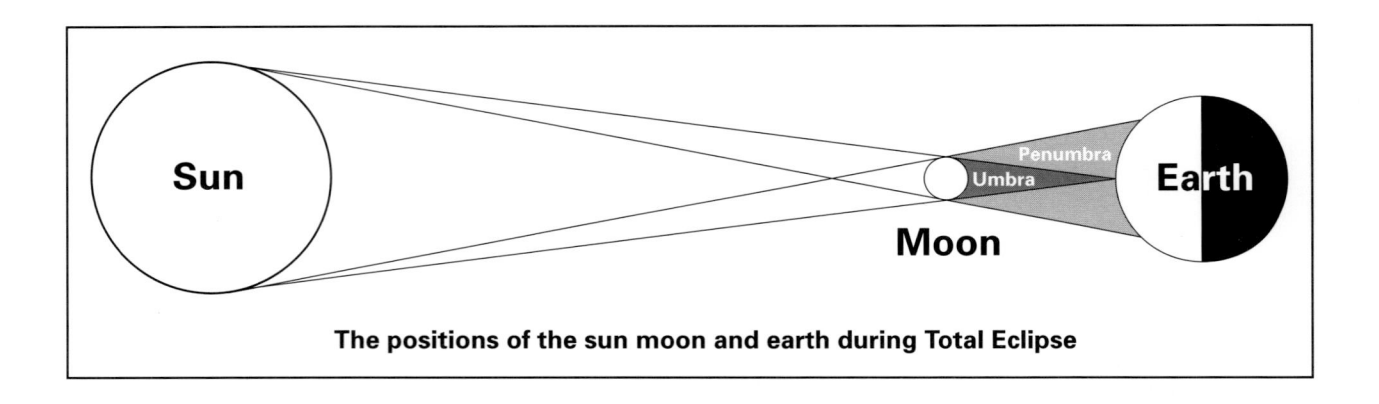

The positions of the sun moon and earth during Total Eclipse

Sometimes just the penumbra strikes the earth, and when this happens we have what is called a **partial eclipse**. To somebody standing on the earth, this looks as though something had taken a bite out of the sun. The sky becomes dull, as though it were a cloudy day.

Sometimes the umbra touches the earth's surface, and the people standing in the shadow will see a **total eclipse** like the one we are expecting in August. This shadow will pass across the earth in a line which is called the path of **totality**.

Standing in the path of totality is very exciting. For just a few moments, the world becomes as black as night and the sun disappears completely. We are able to see all sorts of things that we can't usually see – just what is described later in the book.

The third type of eclipse is called an **annular eclipse**. This happens because the orbit of the moon around the earth is not a circle, but an oval shape called an **ellipse**. It means that sometimes the moon is closer than at other times. If an eclipse happens when the moon is furthest away (we call this the moon's **apogee**) then what we see is a thin ring of light showing around the outer edge of the moon.

Using the information you have just read, can you label the three kinds of eclipses below correctly?

a.

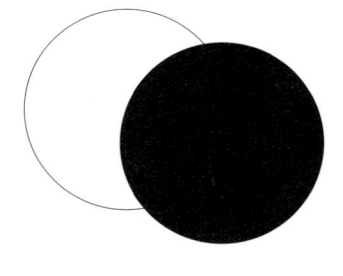

b.

c.

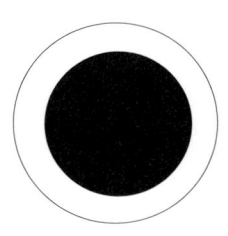

_____   _____   _____

The Path of Totality

This is the grand name given to the line across the earth that the shadow of the eclipse follows. Using the information in the next paragraph, try to draw the path of the 11th August eclipse on the map of the world.

The eclipse will begin in the North Atlantic, just off Canada. It will cross over the Atlantic, and travel over the south west tip of England. Then it will cross the English Channel and pass over Northern France, Germany, Austria and Hungary. It will travel over Romania and Bulgaria, cross over the Black Sea, and move over Turkey, Iraq, Pakistan and India, finally leaving the earth at the Bay of Bengal.

The Saros Series

Did you know that eclipses come in families? The families are called Saros series, and just like the members of families, eclipses in the same Saros series look like each other. This was first noticed about 2500 years ago by some people called the Babylonians. They worked out that eclipses come in groups, or families, with a period of about 18 years between each eclipse.

If you want to see the beginning of a new Saros series, you've only got to wait until July 2011 – the date of a partial eclipse that will begin a series of eclipses that will last for 1400 years! The thing is, you'll have to be on the coast of Antarctica to see it...

Draw the path of totality for the August 1999 Eclipse on this map.

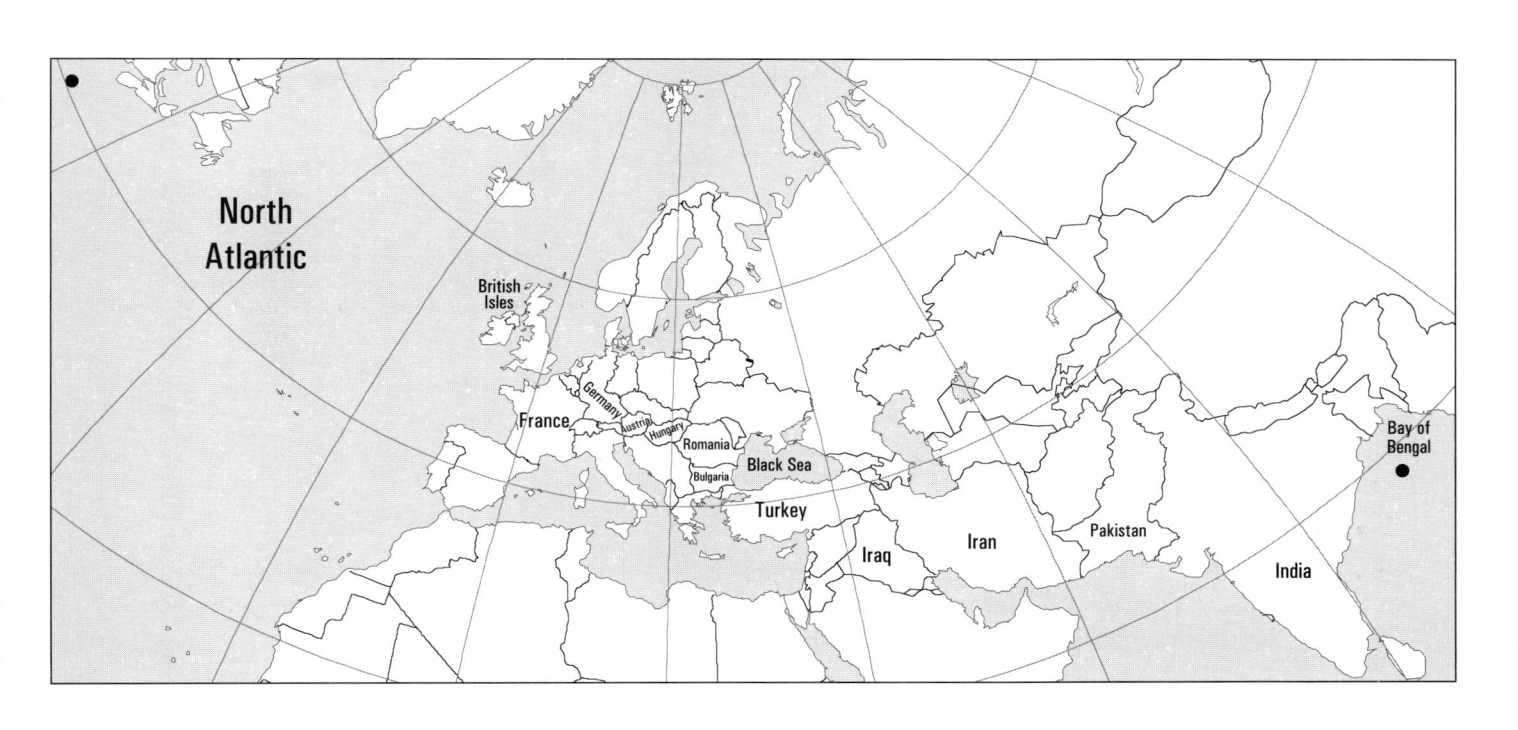

How are you doing so far?

Using the information on the previous pages and/or the glossary, see if you can fill in the blanks with the words below.

The __ __ __ __ __   __ __ __ __ will be the best place for you to watch the eclipse in Great Britain.

A solar eclipse happens when the moon casts a shadow on the __ __ __ __ __.

When the face of the sun is entirely covered we see a __ __ __ __ __ eclipse.

The path of the moon around the earth is called an __ __ __ __ __.

The dark inner shadow cast by the moon is called an __ __ __ __ __,

and the paler outer shadow is called the __ __ __ __ __ __ __ __.

When only a part of the sun is covered, we see a __ __ __ __ __ __ __ eclipse.

People who see the total eclipse are standing in the __ __ __ __ __ __   __ __ __ __ __ __ __ __.

If an eclipse happens when the moon is at its __ __ __ __ __ __, then we see an __ __ __ __ __ __ __ eclipse.

The eclipse of August 1999 will first appear off the coast of
___ ___ ___ ___ ___ ___ .

Eclipses happen in groups called   ___ ___ ___ ___ ___   ___ ___ ___ ___ ___ ___ .

Handy hint:- there are more words here than you need so cross words out as you use them.

Saros Series	annular	path of totality	earth
orbit	south west	planet	Canada	partial
	moon	umbra	penumbra	
sun	eclipse	apogee	total	Scotland

Getting Ready for the Eclipse!

The eclipse will last for about two hours, but the total eclipse will only last for a maximum of two minutes, so it makes sense to have everything you need ready so that you won't miss anything at the time.

1. **This Book!** For all the information and help you'll need to get the most out of the eclipse.

2. **A Compass** So that you can be quite sure where the east and west are.

3. **Provisions!** (meaning food and drink) You might get hungry hanging about waiting for totality, so make sure you're not in a shop buying sweets when everything happens! It's also a good idea to have plenty of drinks as it will be the middle of summer and it could get hot out in the open.

4. **Sunglasses, Sun Cream, Sun Hat** and all that stuff – you don't want to spoil eclipse day by getting sunburnt!

5. **Notebook / Sketchbook** For notes and sketches of what you see. You can also make a note of the things that you'll hear and feel – don't forget that this is a dramatic natural event and affects the whole of the natural world.

6. **Equipment with which to watch the eclipse** There is only one rule you need to remember when watching an eclipse (apart from the obvious ones, like don't stand in the middle of the road to watch it), but it's a VERY IMPORTANT RULE INDEED. You may have noticed that it's very hard to look at the sun – and there's a reason for this. Staring at the sun can result in eye damage, even blindness. So...

Never look directly at the sun without your special viewers !!!

Got that?

The only time that it is safe to look directly at a total eclipse is during the few moments of totality, when the sun is blotted out. But this doesn't mean that you won't be able to see what's going on overhead. There are all sorts of ways you can watch the eclipse in complete safety.

Projection

One of the simplest and safest ways to view the sun is to project its image. It can also be great fun.

Pinhole Camera No.1

You will need two pieces of white card, with a small hole punched through the centre of one of them. By holding them up to the sky so that the sunlight shines through the pinhole onto the second piece of card, you will see a tiny image of the sun, and will be able to follow the eclipse.

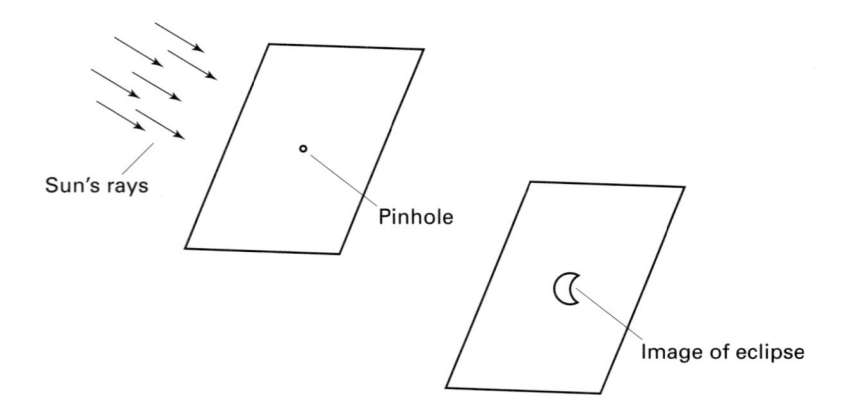

Pinhole Camera No. 2

For a more impressive pinhole camera, you will need a cardboard tube of the kind that people use to send posters or calendars through the post. You'll need to keep the cap that fits in one end, also some white paper, and some sellotape.

Punch a small hole into the cap at one end of the tube, and replace the cap at the other end with a piece of white paper. When you hold the tube up towards the sky so that sunlight shines through the hole, a perfect back-projected image will appear on the paper. But remember not to try and look at the sun through the tube!

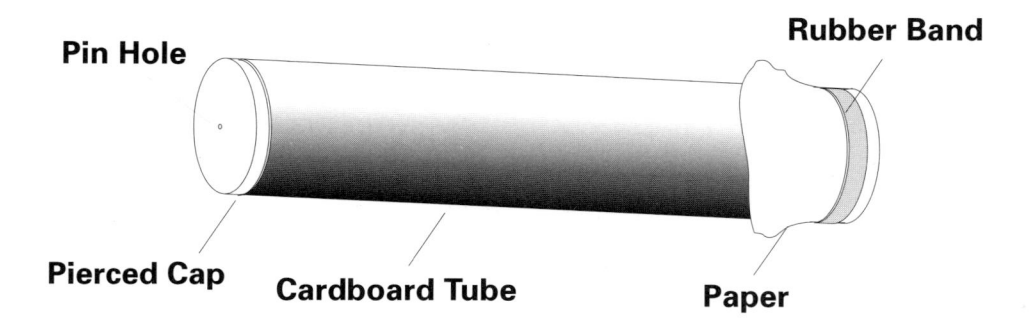

Pin Hole

Rubber Band

Pierced Cap   **Cardboard Tube**   **Paper**

Reflecting the Eclipse

For this you will need a hand mirror and a piece of card cut to the same shape. Make a hole in the card about 15mm across and secure it to the front of the mirror with sellotape. Next, holding the mirror towards the sun, direct the reflected beam on to a shaded surface at about 10 metres distance. You will be able to see an image of the sun, or crescent sun if it's in partial eclipse, cast clearly onto the shaded surface.

For all these ways of watching the eclipse, you will get best results by directing the image onto a shaded surface. A shoebox or something like that would give great results!

Solar Filters

For looking at the sun itself, rather than at its image, you **must** use special protective glasses. You certainly won't be able to make these yourself, and you must use the right kind. There should be plenty of eclipse viewers on sale at the time.

Don't try using sunglasses to watch the eclipse. They aren't designed for looking directly at the sun and will not protect your eyes from the sun's damage. If in doubt, ask a grown-up!

Magnified Viewing

You may want to watch the eclipse through a telescope or binoculars. Certainly, viewing this way you'll be able to pick up all sorts of details of the sun's and moon's surfaces that you might otherwise miss.

Exactly the same rules apply to telescopes and binoculars, **never look directly at the sun without proper protection. The only time it is safe to look at the sun in any way is during totality.**

You can get a special piece of glass to fit over the front end of a telescope or binoculars, which will cut down the Sun's brightness by more than 99% before it reaches your eyes.

WHAT DO WE SEE DURING A TOTAL SOLAR ECLIPSE?

Everyone in Great Britain will be able to see a partial eclipse on 11th August 1999, lasting for about two and a half hours. How much of the sun is covered and how dark it gets will depend on where you are when the eclipse happens – the further south you are, the bigger the eclipse.

Children in Cornwall or South Devon will be the luckiest of all, because they will be right in the path of totality – in other words, they will be able to see the last total solar eclipse of the millennium. This is going to be a very exciting and historic event, so make sure you're up in plenty of time and you've got all the things you'll need.

So, what exactly can you expect to see on the morning of 11th August? Hopefully, at that time of year we should be enjoying clear skies and bright sunshine – ideal weather for watching eclipses. As the eclipse progresses, why not keep a record of how it looks, using the boxes on the next page? You might also want to note down things such as what you can hear, see and feel as the eclipse gets deeper.

But whatever you do, don't forget the golden rule:

Never look directly at the sun without your special viewers !!!

Use the squares below to plot the progress of the total eclipse on 11th August 1999

Time:	Time:	Time:	Time:
Time:	Time:	Time:	Time:

First Contact (About Ten o'Clock)

The stages of an eclipse are known as contacts. The moment when the moon first touches the sun is called the first contact and should happen at about 10 o'clock. (Times will vary depending on where you are). Astronomers call this P1, short for "first penumbral contact". It will seem as though something is beginning to nibble away at the top right-hand corner of the sun.

As the moon's penumbra creeps over the earth, it will feel rather as though the sun is disappearing behind a very big, dark cloud. As the eclipse gets deeper and darker, and you watch the changes taking place overhead, don't forget to notice the changes going on about you in your own world.

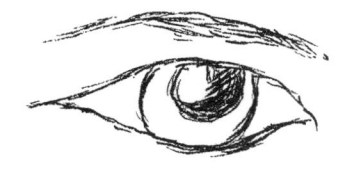

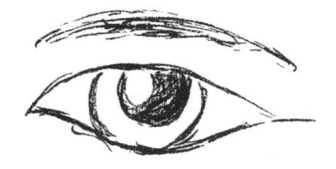

1. **Look.** If you're standing near to some trees, take a look at the sunlight cast through the branches. The criss-cross of leaves and branches will act as dozens of pinhole cameras, like a natural version of the one you've made, and you should be able to see hundreds of tiny crescent shaped suns on the ground.

2. **Feel.** To begin with you might feel a change in the temperature; when the moon covers more than three quarters of the sun's diameter the temperature might fall by 6 degrees C or more. It will feel, as well as look, as though night is falling.

3. **Listen.** Keep your ears open – you should be able to hear the sound of the birds twittering as they prepare to nest for the "night". Eclipses can be very confusing for animals – they think that the day has only lasted for a couple of hours, and it's time to go to bed again! If you are near to farmland, you may see animals heading back to their barns as though it were night time. And look closely at any flowers near where you're standing. They will begin to close as the darkness falls.

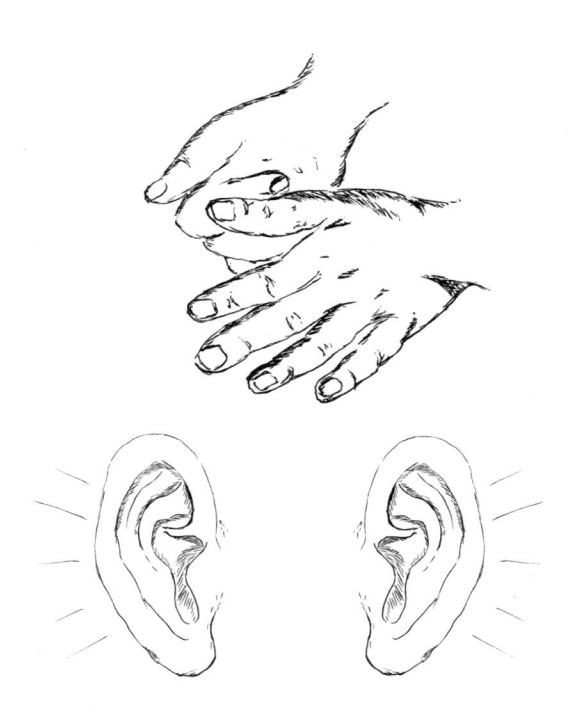

The "bite" in the top right-hand of the sun's disc will grow steadily over the next hour, and the bright circle of the sun will shrink away to a narrow crescent. If you have a telescope (with a protective lens of course) you should be able to pick out details of the usually invisible moon, like its mountains and valleys which will show up against the bright glare of the sun.

Second contact (between ten and fifteen minutes past eleven)

Second contact is when the moon's eastern edge first touches the Sun's eastern edge and the moon covers the sun entirely. It will only be seen along the path of totality. There's a lot to see in the few minutes before totality, so have your pencils ready and be awake! A minute or two before second contact is made look towards the ground for **shadow bands**, ripples of grey light that look a bit like the patterns in the sand after the tide has gone out.

Now look to the west. You should see a great blanket of darkness rushing towards you. This is the umbra of the moon, bringing with it the magical darkness of the total eclipse.

Looking back towards the sun, you should now be able to see one of the most beautiful parts of total eclipse. The crescent of sunlight that is left behind will

↗ Pinhole Effect

Sunlight streaming through the mesh of leaves and branches of trees results in a "pinhole camera" effect — dozens of images on the ground of the clipse taking place overhead. This photograph was taken during the annular eclipse of 10th May 1994 near Toledo, Ohio.

Copyright © Hiram Clawson

suddenly break up into separate points of light which sparkle and shine like jewels. This is caused by the last flashes of sunlight passing through the gaps between the moon's mountains. They are named after an astronomer of the last century, Francis Baily, who described the effect as "a string of bright beads". Ever since they have been known as **Baily's Beads**. Try to draw them later if you see them.

One by one Baily's Beads will disappear, leaving one final bead glowing brighter than the rest, set in a thin ring of light. This has been named the **Diamond Ring**. It will glow brightly for a few seconds, and then will disappear. As it vanishes, the total eclipse begins.

The total eclipse will only last for about two minutes, and there's so much to see! Now it should be safe to take off your special glasses, but **check with a grown-up before you do**. Be ready to put your glasses on again the minute the total eclipse finishes.

So what can you see in these moments of darkness? Much more than you'd think. There are many things going on in our sky all the time that we can't usually see – because the brightness of the sun blinds us! But now, while the sun is covered, we are able to see them.

You will see a very thin circle of glowing red light around the black shadow of the moon. You might notice pink blobs shooting out from this circle – these are called **prominences**, and are jets of gas, hotter than the hottest fire you can imagine, boiling and exploding on the surface of the sun.

Surrounding the circle is the sun's pearly-white corona, blossoming outwards into space, and looking like a great pale flower in the darkness. Using a telescope or binoculars you should be able to see shapes like twisted ribbons, called **coronal streamers**. These are thin streams of gas swirling outwards from the sun.

Now take a look at the rest of the sky. You should be able to see stars and planets, just as you would at night. The horizon will be glowing with a pink, purple or orange light, like a sunset.

Keep your ears open too. If you heard the birds twittering before the total eclipse, now they should have fallen completely silent. This is because they think it's night-time.

Third Contact (after totality)

When a second diamond ring appears, it's time to put your special glasses back on, or look away. This is because the sun is reappearing. As the moon moves back into partial eclipse, you will see all the things you saw leading up to the total eclipse, but in reverse order. Use your compass to look to the east and you will be able to see the moon's umbra rushing away to darken another part of the earth.

Watch and listen over the next hour as the world returns to normal. The "bite" taken out of the sun will grow smaller and smaller. The sky will grow brighter, and the animals and birds will start to bustle again – after a very short night's sleep!

Fourth Contact (about Half Past Twelve)

Fourth contact is made when the moon finally leaves the face of the sun, and we are returned to broad daylight. Congratulations! You have just seen the last total eclipse of the century!

Baily's Beads
The string of jewel-like lights known as Baily's Beads are a result of sunlight streaming through the spaces between the mountains of the moon.

Diamond Ring
The beautiful "Diamond Ring" effect is seen when the last of Baily's Beads shines out just a moment before totality.

Chromosphere ↗

In this photograph of totality the chromosphere of the sun is clearly visible. If you look closely you can see the pink projections of gas rising from the sun's surface.

Copyright © Hiram Clawson

↙ Totality

The glorious moment of totality when the sun's corona is revealed in all its splendour.

Copyright © Hiram Clawson

How much have you remembered?

Using the information on the previous pages, see if you can fill in the blanks.

The moment when the moon first touches the sun is called the first ___ ___ ___ ___ ___ ___ ___ .   Just before totality, we can see ___ ___ ___ ___ ___ ___ ___ ___ ___ ___ ___ on the ground. We will also see a crescent of lights around the moon called ___ ___ ___ ___ ___ ' ___   ___ ___ ___ ___ ___ .   These are caused by the light of the sun shining between the ___ ___ ___ ___ ___ ___ ___ ___ ___ on the moon.

The last of these lights to be seen is called a ___ ___ ___ ___ ___ ___ ___   ___ ___ ___ ___ .   When the sun completely disappears we can see the black disc of the moon surrounded by a pearly white ___ ___ ___ ___ ___ ___ .

Pink crescents of gas called   ___ ___ ___ ___ ___ ___ ___ ___ ___ ___ ___ should be visible.

Third contact marks the end of the __ __ __ __ __ __ __ __ __ __ __ __ .

The sky will brighten and the eclipse is over with the

__ __ __ __ __ __ contact.

Handy hint: There are more words here than you need so cross words out as you use them.

mountains	corona	third	shadow bands
contact	fourth	prominences	partial
Diamond ring	Baily's Beads	total eclipse	

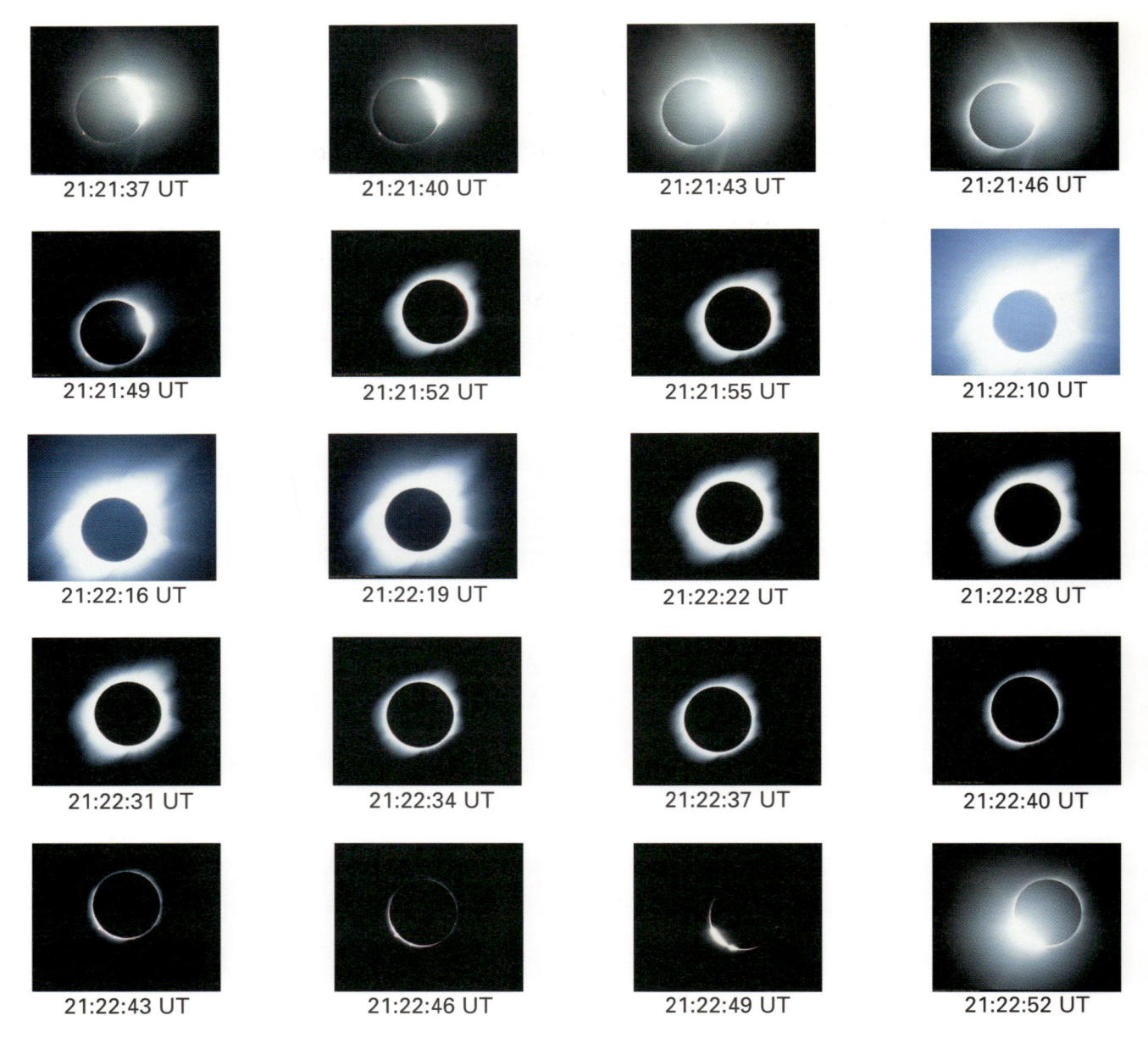

21:21:37 UT	21:21:40 UT	21:21:43 UT	21:21:46 UT
21:21:49 UT	21:21:52 UT	21:21:55 UT	21:22:10 UT
21:22:16 UT	21:22:19 UT	21:22:22 UT	21:22:28 UT
21:22:31 UT	21:22:34 UT	21:22:37 UT	21:22:40 UT
21:22:43 UT	21:22:46 UT	21:22:49 UT	21:22:52 UT

Camera: Minolta X-700 with data back   Film: Kodak slide film ASA 400
Lens: Meade 1000mm f12   Shutter Speeds: Ranging from 1/000 sec to 2 seconds

All images ©1984 Hiram Clawson

SUPERSTITIONS, MYTHS AND LEGENDS

Imagine for a moment that you live a thousand years ago. You and your family live in a small village and depend for your living on farming the land. The most important thing in your life is the sun. It gives you light, and warmth, and you would not be able to grow your crops without it. The wise men of your tribe tell you that the sun is a god. Then one day, without warning, in the middle of a bright sunny morning, the sun disappears! The air grows cold, everything around you is plunged into darkness. What do you think is happening? What do you do? Describe your feelings and what you and the people around you might do . . .

For thousands of years people have looked up at the sky and wondered what an eclipse is. In the twentieth century we know more about the sun, moon and solar system, and understand what causes eclipses. People from the past, who didn't have our powerful telescopes, found other ways of explaining what was going on. Here are some of the things that people from ancient civilisations believed:-

China

Astrologers – people who believe they can tell the future from the stars – have always taken eclipses very seriously, and even today modern astrologers are looking forward to the 1999 eclipse to see what it can tell us about our future.

The ancient Chinese believed that an eclipse was the sign of bad news, and the Emperor Chung K'ang kept two astrologers, called Hsi and Ho, to warn him when an eclipse was due. But Hsi and Ho can't have been very clever, because they chose the night before an eclipse to get drunk – and forgot to warn the emperor that the eclipse was on the way. When Chung K'ang saw the eclipse, he was so furious, he had Hsi and Ho's heads cut off!

The Chinese thought that when an eclipse happened, it was the sun being eaten by a terrible dragon. In order to frighten the dragon away, everybody would go outside and make as much noise as possible. They would pinch babies to make them cry, beat the dogs to make them bark, and bang every pot and pan in the kitchen to try and scare off the monster.

Ancient Greece

Greek history tells a true story about how an eclipse managed to stop a war. On 28th May, 585 BC, two armies called the Medes and the Lydians were in the middle of a fierce battle. They had been at war for five years, and the war showed no signs of stopping. Then, suddenly, the sky became overcast and the sun vanished from sight. The generals of the armies took this as a sign from the Gods that they had to stop fighting, so they made peace there and then!

Africa

An African story tells of how one day, the moon was jealous of the sun's fine golden feathers, and crept up on him to try and steal some feathers for herself. The sun found out, and was so angry that he splashed the moon with mud. This mud stuck to her forever and explains why there are blotchy patches on her face. Ever since, the moon has been trying to get back at the sun, and every so often creeps up and splashes him with mud, covering his face and causing darkness on the earth.

Tahiti

The gentle people of Tahiti didn't think the sun was under attack – in fact they thought the opposite! They believed that the sun and moon were in love and that when an eclipse happened it was the sun stealing a kiss from the moon.

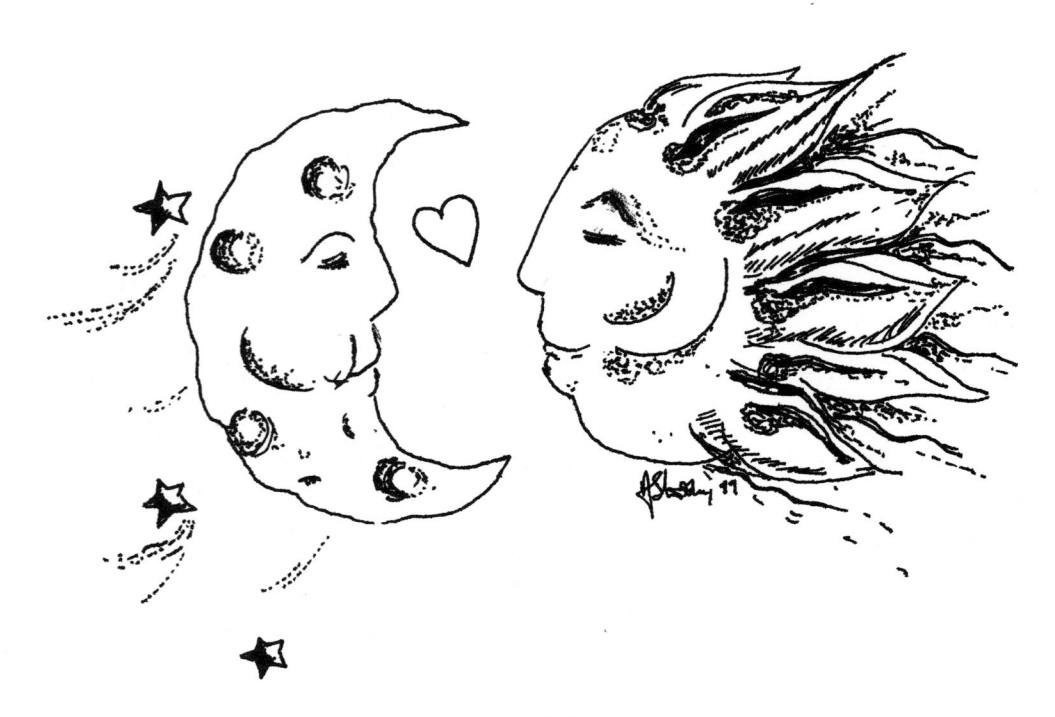

North America

The Chippewa Indians believed that an eclipse happened because the sun was losing its power, and that its fire was going out. They believed that the best way to help was to lie on their backs and fire flaming arrows into the sky. This way, they thought, would help the sun to catch fire again.

South America

The ancient civilisation of the Aztecs had a very bloodthirsty way of dealing with eclipses. They thought that the sun was under attack and needed help to drive away the enemy, so they called upon one of their gods, a magic dog called Xolotl, to come to the aid of the sun. But they believed that Xolotl wouldn't give his help for nothing, so they made a human sacrifice to please him.

India

Indian people believed that the sun was being taken over by an invading force of darkness. In order to drive away the evil spirits, they believed the best thing to do was to go down to the nearest river and stand up to their necks in the water until the eclipse was over.

Many other civilisations believed that someone or something was doing battle with the sun during an eclipse. To the Norsemen, it was a huge wolf, named Skoll. To Mongolian tribes it was Alkha who was responsible, a terrible creature who continued to chase the sun even though his head had been cut off. But whatever these people thought and did about eclipses – the sun always came back!

Now draw your own picture of people reacting to a solar eclipse – or what they imagined was happening in the skies.

Word Square – fill in the squares so that the words below link together.

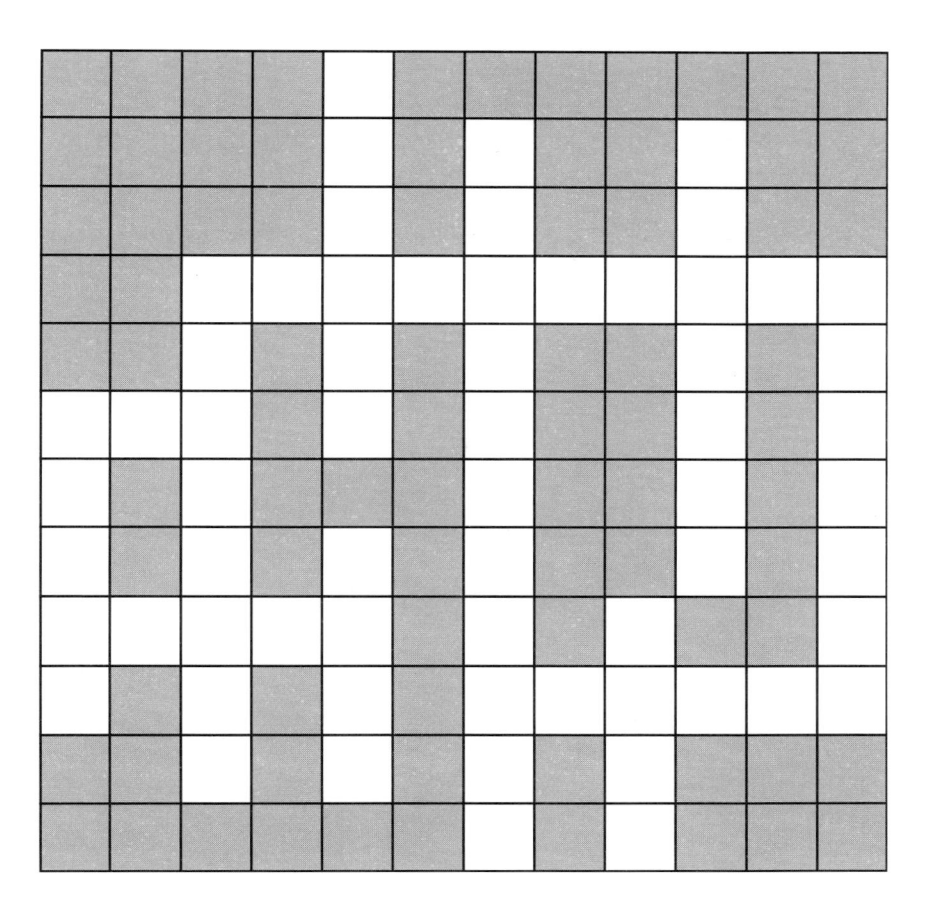

3 LETTERS
Sun

4 LETTERS
Moon
Star

5 LETTERS
Saros
Orbit

6 LETTERS
Corona
Apogee

8 LETTERS
Penumbra

10 LETTERS
Prominence

11 LETTERS
Bailys Beads

Join the dots to find out what the ancient Chinese thought was eating the sun during a solar eclipse!

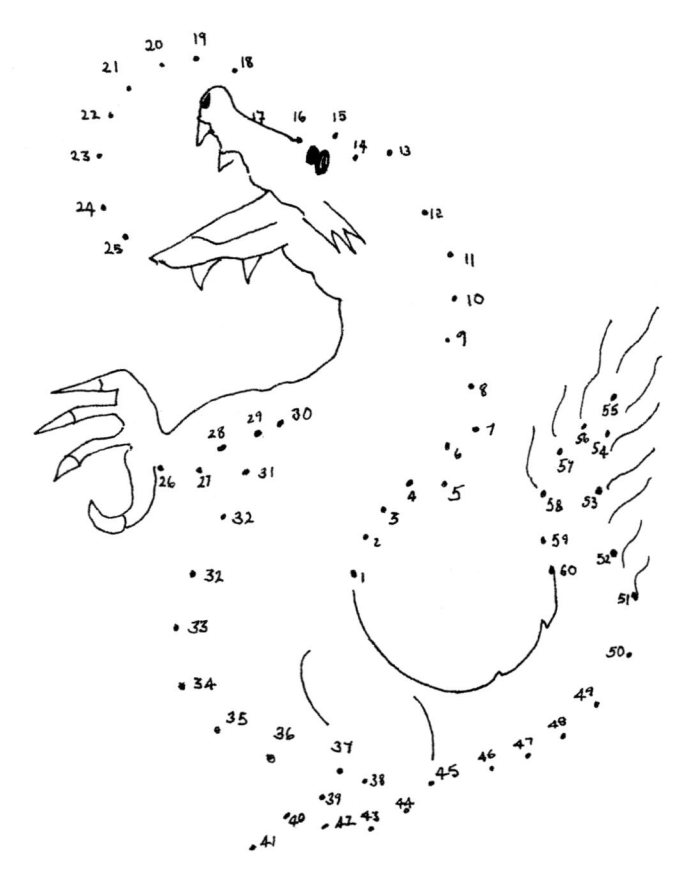

ANSWERS:

Page 3 —

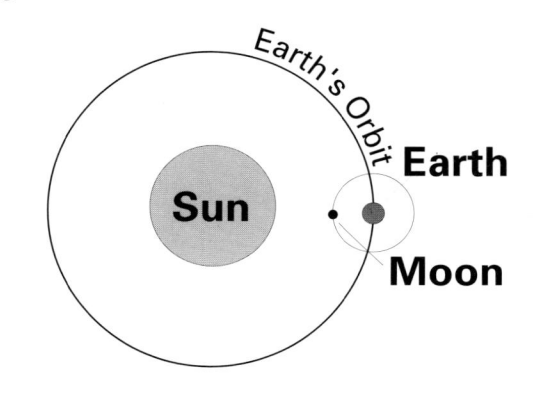

Page 5 —
a) partial   b) total   c) annular

Page 7 —

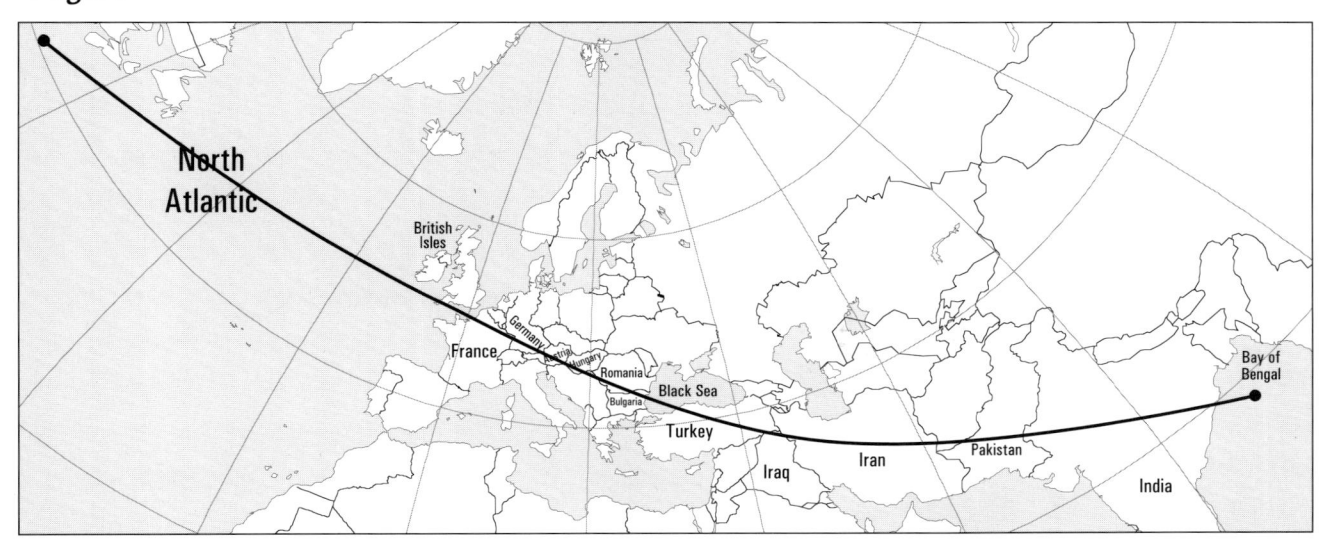

Page 8 —
The <u>south west</u> will be the best place for you to watch the eclipse in Great Britain. A solar eclipse happens when the moon casts a shadow on the <u>earth</u>. When the face of the sun is entirely covered we see a <u>total</u> eclipse. The path of the moon around the earth is called an <u>orbit</u>. The dark inner shadow cast by the moon is called an <u>umbra</u>, and the paler outer shadow is called the <u>penumbra</u>.

When only a part of the sun is covered, we see a <u>partial</u> eclipse. People who ➤

see the total eclipse are standing in the path of totality. If an eclipse happens when the moon is at its apogee, then we see an annular eclipse. The eclipse of August 1999 will first appear off the coast of Canada. Eclipses happen in groups called Saros Series.

Page 24 —
The moment when the moon first touches the sun is called the first contact. Just before totality, we can see shadow bands on the ground. We will also see a crescent of lights around the moon called Baily's Beads. These are caused by the light of the sun shining between the mountains on the moon. The last of these lights to be seen is called a diamond ring.

When the sun completely disappears we can see the black disc of the moon surrounded by a pearly white corona. Pink crescents of gas called prominences should be visible. Third contact marks the end of the total eclipse. The sky will brighten and the eclipse is over with the fourth contact.

Page 37 —

			C					
			O		B		A	
			R		A		N	
		P	R	O	M	I	N	E	N	C	E
		E		N		L		U		C
S	U	N		A		Y		L		L
A		U				S		A		I
R		M		S		B		R		P
O	R	B	I	T		E		M		S
S		R		A		A	P	O	G	E	E
		A		R		D		O	
						S		N	

38

GLOSSARY

Annular Eclipse — An eclipse where the moon passes right in front of the sun, as at total eclipse, but its apparent size is smaller than the sun and a ring of the sun's glare is visible.

Apogee — The point at which the moon is furthest from the earth.

Baily's Beads — A "necklace" of sunlight that appears around the moon just before and after total eclipse.

Contacts — The events in an eclipse. First contact is when the moon's western edge touches the sun's eastern edge; second contact is when the sun is first completely covered; third contact is the moment when totality ends; and fourth contact is when the moon's eastern edge leaves the sun's western edge.

Corona — The outer edge of the sun's atmosphere, extending several sun diameters and which provides the dramatic "light show" of total eclipse.

Diamond Ring — The last "bead" of Baily's Beads showing before total eclipse — also the first to appear afterwards.

Orbit — The elliptical path of one body (earth, moon) around another body (earth, sun).

Path of Totality — A path about 170 miles wide stretching across the surface of the earth, from which a total eclipse can be seen.

Partial Eclipse	An eclipse where the moon passes in front of the sun but only covers a part of the sun's face.
Penumbra	The shadow cast by the moon during partial eclipse.
Prominences	Brilliantly coloured projections of hot gas rising from the sun's surface.
Saros Series	A "family" of eclipses, developing over a period of approximately 1500 years.
Shadow Bands	"Rippled" effects of the sun's light, visible on the ground only during a total eclipse.
Total eclipse	An eclipse where the sun is completely covered by the moon.
Totality	The period during an eclipse when the sun is completely covered by the moon.
Umbra	The shadow cast by the moon during total eclipse.